YOU'RE AWESOME AF.

Here's a book (because it's not like I'm going to tell you to your face)

summersdale

YOU'RE AWESOME AF

An Hachette UK Company
www.hachette.co.uk

Summersdale Publishers Ltd
Part of Octopus Publishing Group Limited
Carmelite House
50 Victoria Embankment
LONDON
EC4Y 0DZ
UK

www.summersdale.com

Printed and bound in China

ISBN: 978-1-78783-543-6

Substantial discounts on bulk quantities of Summersdale books are available to corporations, professional associations and other organizations. For details contact general enquiries: telephone: +44 (0) 1243 771107 or email: enquiries@summersdale.com.

To.....................................

From.................................

ALWAYS BE A FIRST-RATE VERSION OF YOURSELF, INSTEAD OF A SECOND-RATE VERSION OF SOMEBODY ELSE.

Judy Garland

YOU'RE A FLAMINGO IN A FLOCK OF PIGEONS.

YOU'RE AWESOME AF BECAUSE...

you can deal with me
when I'm hangry.

EMBRACE WHO YOU ARE. LITERALLY. HUG YOURSELF. ACCEPT WHO YOU ARE. UNLESS YOU'RE A SERIAL KILLER.

Ellen DeGeneres

AM I GOOD
ENOUGH?
YES I AM.

MICHELLE OBAMA

YOUR
MISTAKES
ARE OTHER
PEOPLE'S
FINEST
MOMENTS.

YOU DESERVE A WHOLE SHEET OF GOLD STARS.

INDEPENDENCE COMES FROM KNOWING WHO YOU ARE AND BEING HAPPY WITH YOURSELF.

Beyoncé

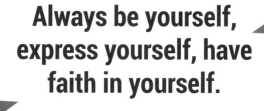

Always be yourself, express yourself, have faith in yourself.

BRUCE LEE

YOU'RE AWESOME AF BECAUSE...

you're always up for
anything and everything.

YOUR TIME IS LIMITED, SO DON'T WASTE IT LIVING SOMEONE ELSE'S LIFE.

Steve Jobs

SOME PEOPLE ARE A DRAIN – YOU'RE A FOUNTAIN.

FIND OUT WHO YOU ARE AND DO IT ON PURPOSE.

Dolly Parton

If you entered the Awesome Olympics, you'd definitely win gold.

SUPERMAN'S GOT NOTHING ON YOU.

I'M TOUGH,
I'M AMBITIOUS
AND I KNOW
EXACTLY WHAT
I WANT. IF THAT
MAKES ME A
B*TCH, OK.

Madonna

I DON'T CARE
WHAT YOU
THINK ABOUT
ME. I DON'T
THINK ABOUT
YOU AT ALL.

Coco Chanel

YOU'RE AWESOME AF BECAUSE...

when you come to a fork
in the road, you pick it
up and start eating.

WHEN LIFE GIVES YOU LEMONS, YOU MAKE A MEAN COCKTAIL.

THEY CAN'T SCARE ME IF I SCARE THEM FIRST.

Lady Gaga

**TAKE CARE NOT
TO LISTEN TO
ANYONE WHO
TELLS YOU WHAT
YOU CAN AND
CAN'T BE IN LIFE.**

Meg Medina

IS IT HARD WORK BEING THE BEST OF THE BEST?

YOU'RE AWESOME
AF BECAUSE...

you are unapologetically you.

DO YOUR THING AND DON'T CARE IF THEY LIKE IT.

Tina Fey

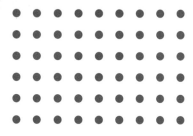

BETTER TO BE A NERD THAN ONE OF THE HERD!

MANDY HALE

YOU'RE THE UMAMI OF PEOPLE.

You
make me
laugh so
hard tears
run down
my leg.

FOLLOW YOUR INNER MOONLIGHT; DON'T HIDE THE MADNESS.

Allen Ginsberg

I AM DIFFERENT.
NOT LESS.

Temple Grandin

THERE'S ORDINARY, AND THEN THERE'S YOU.

YOU'RE AWESOME AF BECAUSE...

you've seen me at my
worst and still like me.

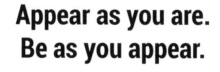

**Appear as you are.
Be as you appear.**

RUMI

ONLY
RECENTLY
HAVE I
REALIZED
THAT BEING
DIFFERENT
IS NOT
SOMETHING
YOU WANT
TO HIDE OR
SQUELCH OR
SUPPRESS.

Amy Gerstler

HATERS GONNA HATE, LEGENDS GONNA LEGEND.

YOU'RE LIKE A PROTON — ALWAYS POSITIVE.

LIFE SHRINKS OR EXPANDS ACCORDING TO ONE'S COURAGE.

Anaïs Nin

BE YOURSELF.
BE TRUE TO
THAT, TO
YOUR HEART.

Nora Roberts

YOU'RE AWESOME AF BECAUSE...

you just are, OK?

YOUR A-GAME IS SO STRONG YOU DON'T EVEN NEED A B-GAME.

BE IN LOVE WITH YOUR LIFE, EVERY DETAIL OF IT.

Jack Kerouac

SELF-RESPECT LEADS TO SELF-DISCIPLINE. WHEN YOU HAVE BOTH FIRMLY UNDER YOUR BELT, THAT'S REAL POWER.

Clint Eastwood

You're made of strong stuff. Like cement.

#LIKEABOSS

KITES RISE
AGAINST NOT
WITH THE WIND.

John Neal

DON'T HIDE FROM WHO YOU ARE.

Rihanna

YOU'RE AWESOME AF BECAUSE...

you always carry snacks.

YOU'RE A
SPRINKLE
DOUGHNUT
IN A WORLD
FULL OF
PLAIN
BAGELS.

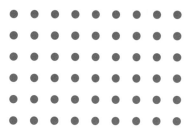

LOVE YOURSELF FIRST, AND EVERYTHING ELSE FALLS INTO LINE.

LUCILLE BALL

THE MOST INCREDIBLE BEAUTY AND THE MOST SATISFYING WAY OF LIFE COME FROM AFFIRMING YOUR OWN UNIQUENESS.

Jane Fonda

IF HUMANS COULD WALK ON WATER, YOU WOULD LEARN TO FLY.

YOU'RE AWESOME
AF BECAUSE...

you live life like you're
starring in your own movie.

**Who you are
authentically
is alright.**

LAVERNE COX

CHERISH
FOREVER
WHAT MAKES
YOU UNIQUE,
'CUZ YOU'RE
REALLY A
YAWN IF
IT GOES.

Bette Midler

YOU'RE AWESOME AF BECAUSE...

you do you better than
anyone else.

YOU MAKE BEYONCÉ LOOK AVERAGE.

PEOPLE HAVE A PROBLEM WITH ME BEING DIFFERENT, BUT THAT PROPELS ME FORWARD IN LIFE.

Mary-Louise Parker

Your daily routine: get up, be amazing, go to bed.

I WAS ONCE AFRAID OF PEOPLE SAYING "WHO DOES SHE THINK SHE IS?" NOW I HAVE THE COURAGE TO STAND AND SAY "THIS IS WHO I AM."

Oprah Winfrey

YOU'RE AWESOME AF BECAUSE...

it's super easy to make you smile
but hard to make you frown.

YOU HAVE TO
BELIEVE IN
YOUR HEART
WHAT YOU
KNOW TO BE
TRUE ABOUT
YOURSELF.
AND LET THAT
BE THAT.

Mary J. Blige

YOU DON'T WORRY ABOUT BEING LIKED. YOU HAVE TO BE YOURSELF.

Vince Vaughn

YOU'RE THE REASON I LOOK AT MY PHONE AND SMILE, AND THEN WALK INTO A POLE.

HOW ARE YOU JUST SO DAMN GOOD?

EMBRACE YOUR WEIRDNESS.

Cara Delevingne

YOU'RE STRONG, YOU'RE A KELLY CLARKSON SONG, YOU'VE GOT THIS.

Jonathan Van Ness

YOU'RE AWESOME AF BECAUSE...

sometimes you have
absolutely no idea what
you're doing, just like me.

YOU ARE GOLD. SOLID GOLD.

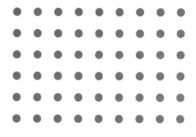

IF YOU CAN'T LOVE YOURSELF, HOW IN THE HELL YOU GONNA LOVE SOMEBODY ELSE?

RuPAUL

YOU ARE YOU. NOW, ISN'T THAT PLEASANT?

Dr Seuss

If you had a
fan club,
I would
definitely
join.

I'D LIKE YOU EVEN IF YOU DIDN'T SHOWER.

YOU DON'T NEED
ANYBODY TO
TELL YOU WHO
YOU ARE OR
WHAT YOU ARE.
YOU ARE WHAT
YOU ARE!

John Lennon

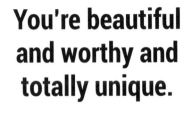

You're beautiful
and worthy and
totally unique.

EMMA STONE

YOU'RE AWESOME AF BECAUSE...

we have enough inside
jokes to fill a novel.

A TALKING DOLPHIN WOULD BE AWESOME, BUT NOT AS AWESOME AS YOU.

TO LOVE ONESELF IS THE BEGINNING OF A LIFELONG ROMANCE.

Oscar Wilde

SOME PEOPLE
SAY YOU ARE
GOING THE
WRONG WAY,
WHEN IT'S
SIMPLY A WAY
OF YOUR OWN.

Angelina Jolie

YOU'RE SO AWESOME YOU PROBABLY SWEAT GLITTER.

YOU'RE AWESOME
AF BECAUSE...

you have all the answers,
just like Google.

YOU ARE YOU
BECAUSE YOU
ARE YOU AND
YOU WERE
MEANT TO BE
YOU, SO BE
YOU PROUDLY.

Tegan Quin

WANTING TO BE SOMEONE ELSE IS A WASTE OF WHO YOU ARE.

Kurt Cobain

EVERYTHING YOU TOUCH TURNS TO AWESOME.

You're better than hot buttered toast.

WE MUST OVERCOME THE NOTION THAT WE MUST BE REGULAR... IT ROBS YOU OF THE CHANCE TO BE EXTRAORDINARY.

Uta Hagen

YOU CAN'T GIVE UP! WHEN YOU GIVE UP, YOU'RE LIKE EVERYBODY ELSE.

Chris Evert

IN HIGH SCHOOL, WERE YOU VOTED "MOST LIKELY TO ALWAYS BE AWESOME"?

YOU'RE AWESOME AF BECAUSE...

you're a limited edition.

THERE'S
A WHOLE
CATEGORY
OF PEOPLE
WHO MISS
OUT BY NOT
ALLOWING
THEMSELVES
TO BE WEIRD
ENOUGH.

Alain de Botton

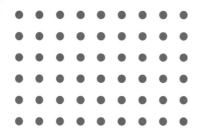

STOP HOLDING YOUR TRUTH; SPEAK YOUR TRUTH. BE YOURSELF. IT'S THE HEALTHIEST WAY TO BE.

TIFFANY HADDISH

I BET
YOU WERE
JUST BORN
AWESOME.

YOU COULD DEFINITELY SURVIVE A ZOMBIE APOCALYPSE.

_____

YOU ONLY GET
TO BE GOOD
BY MAKING
MISTAKES,
AND YOU ONLY
GET TO BE
REAL BY BEING
IMPERFECT.

Julianne Moore

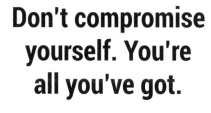

Don't compromise yourself. You're all you've got.

JANIS JOPLIN

YOU'RE AWESOME AF BECAUSE...

no one does gossip like you do.

WHEN YOU EMBRACE YOUR DIFFERENCE... THAT'S WHEN YOU START TO SHINE.

Bethenny Frankel

YOU KEEP
ALL MY
SECRETS.

THE TYPICAL
EXPRESSION
OF OPENING
FRIENDSHIP
WOULD BE
SOMETHING
LIKE, "WHAT?
YOU TOO? I
THOUGHT I WAS
THE ONLY ONE."

C. S. Lewis

In school sports, I would definitely pick you first.

YOU DO
YOU SO
VERY,
VERY
WELL.

BE LOUD ABOUT THE THINGS THAT ARE IMPORTANT TO YOU.

Karen Walrond

I JUST DON'T BELIEVE IN PERFECTION. BUT I DO BELIEVE IN SAYING, "THIS IS WHO I AM AND LOOK AT ME NOT BEING PERFECT!"

Kate Winslet

YOU'RE AWESOME
AF BECAUSE...

you make bad energy
disappear like magic!

YOU SHOULD
HAVE YOUR
OWN SHOW.
I WOULD
DEFINITELY
WATCH IT.

YOU CANNOT CHANGE WHAT YOU ARE, ONLY WHAT YOU DO.

Philip Pullman

TAKING INTO ACCOUNT THE PUBLIC'S REGRETTABLE LACK OF TASTE, IT IS INCUMBENT UPON YOU NOT TO FIT IN.

Janeane Garofalo

"AVERAGE" IS A WORD USED FOR OTHER PEOPLE.

YOU'RE AWESOME
AF BECAUSE...

you're officially the funniest
person on the planet.

I HAVE
INSECURITIES
OF COURSE,
BUT I DON'T
HANG OUT
WITH ANYONE
WHO POINTS
THEM OUT
TO ME.

Adele

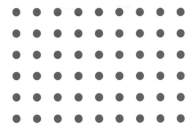

HOWEVER DIFFICULT LIFE MAY SEEM, THERE IS ALWAYS SOMETHING YOU CAN DO AND SUCCEED AT.

STEPHEN HAWKING

AWESOME CALLED – IT WANTS ITS TITLE BACK.

I'm so happy I don't have to pay to hang out with you. But I would.

NEVER DULL YOUR SHINE FOR SOMEBODY ELSE.

Tyra Banks

ONE CAN NEVER CONSENT TO CREEP WHEN ONE FEELS AN IMPULSE TO SOAR.

Helen Keller

IF EVERYONE WERE LIKE YOU, THE WORLD WOULD BE FREE OF ALL PROBLEMS.

YOU'RE AWESOME AF BECAUSE...

you're the cheese to my macaroni.

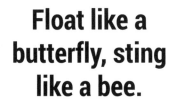

**Float like a
butterfly, sting
like a bee.**

MUHAMMAD ALI

JUST BE COMFORTABLE WITH WHO YOU ARE.

Chris Pratt

WHEN
WE HUG,
I SECRETLY
HOPE YOUR
AWESOMENESS
IS RUBBING
OFF ON ME.

IF YOU AND A PUPPY WERE IN AN AWESOME COMPETITION, YOU WOULD DEFINITELY WIN.

OWNING
OUR STORY
AND LOVING
OURSELVES
THROUGH THAT
PROCESS IS THE
BRAVEST THING
WE'LL EVER DO.

Brené Brown

THE PRIVILEGE OF A LIFETIME IS BEING WHO YOU ARE.

Joseph Campbell

YOU'RE AWESOME AF BECAUSE...

you always message me back
(even if it's super late).

YOU MUST MAKE BABIES SMILE ALL THE TIME.

!

SOME
PEOPLE ARE
SO MUCH
SUNLIGHT TO
THE SQUARE
INCH.

Walt Whitman

JUST BE YOURSELF – THERE IS NO ONE BETTER.

Taylor Swift

You're like novelty socks – cool, in your own special way.

YOU'RE SO
AWESOME
YOU
PROBABLY
DO
CROSSWORD
PUZZLES IN
PERMANENT
MARKER.

**DON'T YOU EVER
LET A SOUL IN
THE WORLD
TELL YOU THAT
YOU CAN'T BE
EXACTLY WHO
YOU ARE.**

Lady Gaga

YOU'RE ALWAYS WITH YOURSELF, SO YOU MIGHT AS WELL ENJOY THE COMPANY.

Diane von Fürstenberg

YOU'RE AWESOME AF BECAUSE...

when you talk, everybody listens.

YOU MAKE

AWESOME

LOOK EASY.

NORMAL IS NOT SOMETHING TO ASPIRE TO; IT'S SOMETHING TO GET AWAY FROM.

JODIE FOSTER

I AVOID LOOKING FORWARD OR BACKWARD, AND TRY TO KEEP LOOKING UPWARD.

Charlotte Brontë

ANYONE CAN BE COOL, BUT AWESOME TAKES PRACTICE.

YOU'RE AWESOME AF BECAUSE...

you always look on the bright side.

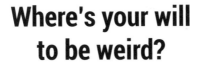

Where's your will to be weird?

JIM MORRISON

TO BE ONE,
TO BE UNITED
IS A GREAT
THING. BUT TO
RESPECT THE
RIGHT TO BE
DIFFERENT IS
MAYBE EVEN
GREATER.

Bono

YOU'RE
SO WEIRD.
NEVER
CHANGE.

Is there anything you can't do?

I PROMISE YOU
THAT EACH AND
EVERY ONE OF
YOU IS MADE TO
BE WHO YOU ARE.

Selena Gomez

BE YOURSELF.
YOU'RE OK.
AND IT REALLY
DOESN'T MATTER
WHAT OTHER
PEOPLE THINK.

Taylor Schilling

I'VE SEEN YOU AT YOUR WORST AND YOU'RE STILL AWESOME.

YOU'RE AWESOME
AF BECAUSE...

we can be weird AF together!

NOTHING IS IMPOSSIBLE. THE WORD ITSELF SAYS "I'M POSSIBLE!"

Audrey Hepburn

IN ORDER TO BE IRREPLACEABLE ONE MUST ALWAYS BE DIFFERENT.

Coco Chanel

YOU MAKE
ME WANT
TO BE MORE
AWESOME.

WINNING AT LIFE IS YOUR M.O.

NORMAL IS NOTHING MORE THAN A CYCLE ON A WASHING MACHINE.

Whoopi Goldberg

PURSUE THE
THINGS YOU
LOVE DOING,
AND THEN DO
THEM SO WELL
THAT PEOPLE
CAN'T TAKE
THEIR EYES
OFF YOU.

Maya Angelou

YOU'RE AWESOME AF BECAUSE...

your laugh is contagious!

YOU ALWAYS
KNOW THE
RIGHT THING
TO SAY.

THE MOST
BEAUTIFUL THING
YOU CAN WEAR
IS CONFIDENCE.

BLAKE LIVELY

I ALWAYS HAD THE ABILITY TO SAY NO. THAT'S HOW I CALLED MY OWN SHOTS.

Sidney Poitier

IF YOU WERE
A NINTENDO
64 GAME,
YOU'D BE
MARIO KART.

YOU'RE AWESOME
AF BECAUSE...

you can lead a horse to
water AND make it drink.

BE YOURSELF,
DO YOUR OWN
THING AND
WORK HARD. THE
RIGHT PEOPLE –
THE ONES WHO
REALLY BELONG
IN YOUR LIFE –
WILL COME TO
YOU. AND STAY.

Will Smith

If you're interested in finding out more about our books, find us on Facebook at **Summersdale Publishers** and follow us on Twitter at **@Summersdale**.

www.summersdale.com